LANGUAGE DEVELOPMENT ACHIEVEMENT ACTIVITIES

Robert L. Doan, Ed.D.

Robert L. Doan, Ed.D., has been involved in education for more than twenty years as a teacher of preschool, elementary, and junior high students, and as an undergraduate and graduate professor. He has written numerous articles on Early Childhood Education and reading, and has produced a film on perceptual-motor training.

Dr. Doan received his doctorate from Ball State University, Muncie, Indiana, and was associate professor of education at Indiana University-Purdue University in Fort Wayne. He is presently professor of Early Childhood Education at The University of South Alabama, Mobile.

EARLY CHILDHOOD ACHIEVEMENT UNITS

The Center for Applied Research in Education, Inc.
West Nyack, New York   10994

Printed in the United States of America

ABOUT THE
"EARLY CHILDHOOD ACHIEVEMENT UNITS"

The purpose of the "Early Childhood Achievement Units" is to provide meaningful and worthwhile activities for the early childhood education classroom. Together, the six units in the series offer over 250 classroom-tested activities ready for immediate use as core components of the curriculum or as a means to introduce new concepts, reinforce concepts being taught, or culminate a study.

Each Achievement Unit is designed to meet the special needs of children in a specific educational area. The six units and the primary objectives for which they are intended are:

Arts and Crafts Achievement Activities
- to provide opportunities for pencil (crayon) and paper activities
- to develop spatial relationships
- to develop color and shape discrimination
- to develop eye-hand coordination
- to develop listening skills and the ability to follow directions
- to provide opportunities for creative expression

Body Management Achievement Activities
- to develop gross motor and fine motor skills
- to develop balance and coordination
- to develop eye-hand coordination
- to develop spatial relationships
- to develop tactile-kinesthetic skills
- to provide opportunities to enjoy the pleasures of movement

Language Development Achievement Activities
- to develop listening skills
- to provide opportunities to use language skills
- to increase vocabularies
- to develop awareness of sequential events

3

- to develop a fondness for storytelling
- to develop a fondness for books and an eagerness for reading

Number Readiness Achievement Activities
- to develop understanding of sets
- to develop an understanding of numbers
- to develop an understanding of numerals
- to develop shape and form discrimination
- to introduce basic mathematics vocabulary
- to nurture children's curiosity into numerical inquiry

Science Discovery Achievement Activities
- to provide inquiry into natural phenomena
- to develop understanding about plants and animals
- to provide problem-solving opportunities
- to introduce the bases of scientific inquiry
- to provide opportunities to enjoy nature

Social Living Achievement Activities
- to learn about self
- to learn about families and relatives
- to learn about neighbors and friends
- to learn about communities and community helpers
- to learn about people around the world
- to learn about jobs and responsibilities

The activities in the "Early Childhood Achievement Units" are tailored to coincide with the developmental needs of young children. Some are designed to provide basics in academic areas while others are oriented toward the socio-emotional needs of children. Whether the children are four-year-olds in a nursery school or day care center or fives and sixes in a kindergarten or first grade, the activities can be easily adapted to a wide range of individual and group needs by varying the degree of assistance provided by the teacher.

And all activities are carefully organized for easy use. Each is given a distinct title and is designated for individual, small group, and/or large group use. Each states a primary purpose (secondary purposes are not stated, but are usually obvious), lists needed supplies, provides explicit directions, and offers follow-up suggestions. Moreover, many activities include illustrations as a helpful supplement to directions.

Each Achievement Unit also includes a special section entitled "For the Teacher." This provides a variety of practical teaching tips and source materials for the particular area of instruction.

The activities in these "Early Childhood Achievement Units" have been used successfully in primary grades, kindergartens, nursery schools, child care centers, Montessori schools, and in special education classes. They can be used effectively with nearly all young children with adjustments to meet individual needs.

Robert L. Doan

CONTENTS

LANGUAGE DEVELOPMENT ACHIEVEMENT ACTIVITIES

AUDITORY PERCEPTION

> *These activities give the teacher opportunities to observe the children's skill levels in auditory involvement.*

LISTENING SKILLS

> *These activities provide a variety of auditory experiences, ranging from concrete to abstract, from simple to complex.*

VISUALS

These activities offer many ways to enliven language development. Use them with imagination to make stories come alive.

POETRY AND FINGERGAMES

These activities demonstrate several ways to utilize rhyming stories.

READING STORIES

These activities suggest ways to lengthen children's attention spans, help children understand story lines, gain knowledge from stories, and appreciate classical children's literature.

STORY TELLING

These activities suggest ways to tell stories instead of reading stories, thus providing alternative methods to enhance literature.

WORD CONCEPTS

These activities suggest ways to increase children's vocabularies and understandings of abstract and/or complex concepts.

PROMINENT PERSONALITIES

This activity is presented as a technique you may use to present literature about famous people.

SETTING THE SCENE FOR SPEAKING

Children need many opportunities for developing their language. The preceding activities "set the scene."

SPEAKING IN SENTENCES

Children need to develop communicative skills that express complete thoughts. These activities offer experiences that create a need for speaking in complete sentences.

LETTERS, LETTER SOUNDS, AND PRINTING

These activities are for children mature enough to begin pencil-paper and beginning reading activities.

FOR THE TEACHER

These references will help you locate and utilize materials that support language development activities.

EFFECTIVE USE OF THESE ACTIVITIES

Language Development Achievement Activities presents a variety of worthwhile activities to help children develop skills in the language arts. In implementing these activities, the main emphasis should be placed on a balanced approach to language development appropriate to the children's developmental level. Very young children, for example, should not be involved in letter recognition activities prior to their readiness for such activities.

It is also suggested that the activities be varied frequently. Children should enjoy and cherish their involvement in children's literature, discussion activities, constructing puppets and other visual aids, the listening games, the recognition of letters, and being able to print their own names. It is well known that happy association with an act or idea produces lasting results of consequence.

Some further suggestions for the use of these language development activities are: (1) if the activity requires a length of time beyond children's ability, be sure to divide the activity into several sessions, (2) plan the activity so it is not interrupted by lunch or dismissal, (3) plan clean-up time and equipment in advance, and (4) remember that children have accidents. Treat accidents like accidents.

The activities in this handbook are presented in categories that encompass a wide range of skills. While it is recommended that you select activities in various categories rather than use all the activities in one category prior to using any activities in the next category, the categories themselves have some priority of difficulty. For example, some four and five-year-olds will not be ready for printing activities. However, the same children will be ready for all kinds of stories and fingergames and poems.

The categories of language development activities are: Auditory Perception, Listening Skills, Visuals, Poetry and Fingergames, Reading Stories, Telling Stories, Word Concepts, Prominent Personalities, Setting the Scene for Speaking, Speaking in Sentences, Letters, Letter Sounds and Printing.

Guidelines for selecting children's literature and a variety of resources for language development activities are presented in a special section, "For the Teacher," at the end of the handbook.

LANGUAGE DEVELOPMENT ACHIEVEMENT ACTIVITIES

Individual *
Small Group
Large Group

Title: **CHECKING ACUITY**

Purpose: To screen children for hearing loss.

Materials Needed: Watch (that ticks loudly)

Procedure:

Have each child sit in a chair facing a plain wall. Then say to the child, "I'm going to place this watch by your ear. If you hear the watch ticking, raise your hand." Be sure the child knows what you mean by ". . . raise your hand." Next move the watch slowly away from the child's ear. Say to the child, "When you no longer hear the ticking, put your hand down."

Most children will be able to hear the watch's ticking from 8 to 12 inches, but this, of course, depends upon the loudness of the watch. Be alert for the child who cannot hear the ticking up close to the ear.

Check both of the child's ears.

Follow-up: Refer children who you suspect have a hearing loss. Better safe than sorry!

Title: **IDENTIFYING SOUNDS**

Purpose: To develop skill in matching auditory clues with visual stimuli.

Materials Needed: Tape recorder
                      Audio tape
                      Pictures cut from old magazines
                        such as: wrist watch
                                  lawn mower
                                  telephone
                                  dishwasher
                                  truck
                                  typewriter
                                  drum

Procedure:

Take the tape recorder home some weekend and tape about 15 seconds of each of the sounds suggested by the pictures listed above.

At school, place the cut-out pictures on the surface of a table. Then have a child or a small group of children view the pictures before you start the tape recorder. After the children have looked the pictures over, start the recorder and as each segment is played, have the children remove the corresponding picture.

Follow-up: Record sounds from different areas of the community: park sounds, traffic sounds, zoo sounds, farm sounds, school sounds, etc. Make up packets of pictures to go with each of the audio tapes.

Title: **RECALLING AUDITORY INFORMATION**

Purpose: To reinforce auditory memory.

Materials Needed: None

Procedure:

Gather the children about you in a circle and play "categories." You select a category such as "pets." Ask each child in turn to tell the name of an animal and the sound it makes (kitty-meow, cow-moo). Other categories that might stimulate recall are favorite TV shows, boys' names, girls' names, favorite food, favorite desserts, favorite games, favorite toys.

Follow-up: When children appear adept at recall, try teaching them short poems or fingergames. They love the rhythm and rhyme of poetry.

Excellent sources of poems and fingergames are old and new magazines, such as *Highlights for Children, Instructor, Teacher, Early Years, Young Children, Elementary English, Family Circle, Jack & Jill,* and *Ranger Rick's Nature Magazine.*

A good book for resource is: LET'S DO FINGERPLAYS, Grayson, Marion. 1962. Robert B. Luce, Inc., 200 "N" Street, N.W., Washington, D.C. 20036.

Title: **AUDITORY SCREENING**

Purpose: To develop the ability to discount irrelevant auditory stimulus.

Materials Needed: Ditto master
                        Ditto paper
                        Radio or record player with record
                        Crayons, 3 per child: red, blue, yellow

Procedure:

Prepare a ditto master similar to the sample below. Duplicate the ditto and distribute the copies to the children. Give each child three crayons.

Explain to the children that you are going to give them directions, but that you will deliberately play some music while you are giving instructions. Tell them that their job is to pay no attention to the music, but rather to listen intently to your directions. Before you start the music, give the children a sample of directions. Say, "Pick up your red crayon and color the star red." Now, start the music in the background and give the children directions on how you would like to have them color the various items on the paper.

Follow-up: You may upgrade the complexity of this activity by giving different directions to boys and girls. The children will thus have to screen irrelevant background music *and* screen irrelevant instructions.

Sample: "Girls, pick up your yellow crayon and color the crescent moon yellow. Boys, color the balloon red."

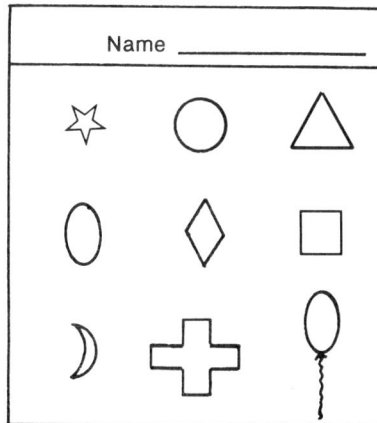

15

Title: **PLEASURE LISTENING**

Purpose: To provide pleasure through music, stories, or poetry.

Materials Needed: Record player
                        Recordings of children's stories, poems, or music

Procedure:

During snack time, clean-up time, rest period, or even during play period, play a background of children's music or poetry. This type of listening can have a calming effect on groups of children and as a result provide a quieter environment for classroom activities.

Follow-up: Solicit records from your classroom children's parents for playing at school.

Individual
Small Group   *
Large Group

Title: **PRODUCTIVE LISTENING**

Purpose: To develop critical listening skills.

Materials Needed: Classical storybook
                        Art paper
                        Crayons

Procedure:

Gather the children around you in a "listening area." Read to them a classical children's story such as *Peter Rabbit* or *The Three Little Pigs.* As you read the story, pause to ask the children "productive" questions; that is, questions that do not require story recall, but rather questions that require projected answers. Such questions might start like: "What

16

would happen if we . . . ?" "If we lived in a house of straw, what might . . . ?"

Follow-up: This is an outstanding opportunity to allow children to express their thoughts through art. For example, you might finish reading a story to the children and confront them with a "What if . . ." questions and ask them to draw or color their responses.

.

Individual   *
Small Group   *
Large Group   *

Title: **MEANINGFUL LISTENING: HOUSEHOLD SOUNDS**

Purpose: To develop listening skills in identifying specific noises.

Materials Needed: Tape recorder

Procedure:

Take a tape recorder home over the weekend and record many, many short (ten seconds) segments of common household noises: such as, sweeper, toaster, alarm clock, radio, TV, dishwasher, pots and pans, silverware, outside traffic sounds, family conversations, garage door, meal-time sounds.

Take the recorder back to school, and during a listening time or discussion time, play the tape for the children and have them identify the noises.

Follow-up: Cautiously, encourage the children to identify the noises verbalizing in complete sentences. Do not push for complete sentences to the extent that children would rather not participate.

17

Title: **MEANINGFUL LISTENING:
FOLLOWING DIRECTIONS**

Purpose: To promote skill in listening to and following directions.

Materials Needed: None

Procedure:

Gather a small group of children around you in a "listening area." Explain to the children that you are going to give them a series of things to do to see if they can do all the things they are asked to do. Then have one child at a time stand and face you. Establish strong eye contact with the child and give him/her a series of three directions to follow. While giving the instructions, reinforce the auditory communications by holding up one finger during the first instruction, two fingers during the second instruction, and three fingers during the third instruction. For example, "Tommy, walk to the chalkboard (holding up one finger). Pick up a chalk eraser (holding up two fingers), and skip back to me" (holding up three fingers).

Follow-up: Extend the directions to the ability levels of the children by increasing the complexity and/or number of instructions.

Title: **DISCRIMINATIVE LISTENING:**
ABSTRACT SOUNDS

Purpose: To develop auditory perception skills.

Materials Needed: 12 Pringle's cans (or suitable substitute)
6 different kinds of matter to put into Pringle's cans (rice, beans, paper clips, thumbtacks, marbles, straight pins)
Paper and glue

Procedure:

Prepare the cans by lining the inside of the lids with paper so the children cannot see through them.

Next, put equal amounts of rice in each of two cans. Continue with the beans, paper clips, and so on. You now have six pairs of cans that should make nearly identical noises when rattled.

Demonstrate to the children how the cans with differing matter produce differing sounds. Next demonstrate how you can mix the twelve cans, then pair them by sound.

The children may check their accuracy by removing the lids and checking the contents.

Follow-up: Select one can from each of the six pairs. See if the children can place the six cans in order according to the weight of the contents. For example, marbles first, then paper clips, tacks, beans, rice, pins.

19

Title: **SOUND DISCRIMINATION: PIANO TONES**

Purpose: To develop auditory discrimination skills.

Materials Needed: Piano or other instrument, e.g., guitar, autoharp, pitchpipe

Procedure:

Gather a small group of children (or individual) near the piano. Explain and demonstrate to the children the concepts of "higher notes" and "lower notes." Play a high note and a low note that are very obviously far apart. Then gradually play notes that are nearer and nearer to each other. When the children understand the concept, let them take turns telling whether the second note played is higher or lower than the first note.

As the children become skilled at discriminating the tones, play notes closer and closer together to increase the need for sharp discrimination.

Follow-up: Introduce "alike" tones. Play two notes next to each other on the piano, then play the same note twice. Let the children decide if the combinations are "alike" or "different."

Title: **AESTHETIC LISTENING:**
MOVEMENT EXPRESSION

Purpose: To promote creative responses to listening experiences.

Materials Needed: Record player
Rhythmic recording of music

Procedure:

Gather the children into an open area where they can
move about without running into one another. Then, before
playing the rhythmic recording, remind them that they must
listen to the music carefully to "feel" the rhythm. Have one
or two children demonstrate how to listen to the music and
then move their bodies freely and rhythmically to the beat.
Next, play the recording for all the children as they respond
freely.

Follow-up: On a homemade drum or tom-tom, play various
beats. Have the children listen carefully to the beat and then
respond. Several suggested beats are: (ONE, two, three, four),
(ONE, two, three), (ONE, two, THREE, four).

21

Individual

Small Group *

Large Group *

Title: **AESTHETIC LISTENING: GRAPHIC EXPRESSION**

Purpose: To promote creative response to listening experiences.

Materials Needed: Art paper, 1 sheet per child
Crayons *or* finger paints
Record player and rhythmic recording

Procedure:

Perform an experiment with the children to determine whether they express themselves differently when using crayons and/or paints with musical background as opposed to no musical background.

On the first day, distribute the art supplies to the children. Instruct them to use their crayons and/or paints to make a picture. On a following day, distribute the art supplies and give the children the same instructions as the previous day. Tell the children that you are going to play a record while they are doing their work, but don't explain why you are playing the record.

Compare the graphic products.

Follow-up: Make a third comparison. Instruct the children just as you did on the second day, but play a dreary recording of chamber music or a composition such as the *Volga Boatmen.* (Recordings are available from public libraries.) Compare all three drawings.

Individual *

Small Group *

Large Group

Title: **LISTENING PANTOMIME: ONE CONCEPT**

Purpose: To develop listening skills while participating in spontaneous dramatics.

Materials Needed: None

22

Procedure:

Gather the children into an area where there is space for movement. Then, give the children, individually or in small groups, simple suggestions for acting out an activity. For example:

> "Show how you walk in deep snow."
> "Show how you wade in very cold water."
> "Show how you set the table."
> "Show how you walk barefooted on a hot sidewalk."
> "Show how you sweep the porch."

Follow-up: When children feel uninhibited in dramatizing, let individuals act out an activity and let other children guess what the action is.

Individual   *
Small Group *
Large Group

Title: **LISTENING PANTOMIME: DUAL CONCEPT**

Purpose: To develop listening skills while participating in spontaneous dramatics.

Materials Needed: None

Procedure:

Gather the children into an area where there is space for movement. Then give the children, individually or in small groups, suggestions for acting out a conditional pantomime. For example, say, "Act like elephants walking . . ." (when the children start walking like elephants, add the condition ". . . barefooted on a hot sidewalk."

Follow-up: Some other suggestions are:

Subject	*Condition*
Train . . .	. . . chugging up hill
Swimming . . .	. . . in very cold water
Kite . . .	. . . on a calm day
Kite . . .	. . . on a windy day
Leaves . . .	. . . blowing in the wind
Roller skates . . .	. . . skating for the first time
Bike . . .	. . . riding on a two-wheeler for the first time

Title: **PUPPET STAGE**

Purpose: To prepare a setting for children to use puppets.

Materials Needed: Card table
                         Large towels or pieces of cloth, 2

Procedure:

Unfold the legs of a card table and place the card table on its side. Then drape towels over the upper legs with the towels hanging downward on the sides. These towels block the view of children using puppets inside the "stage."

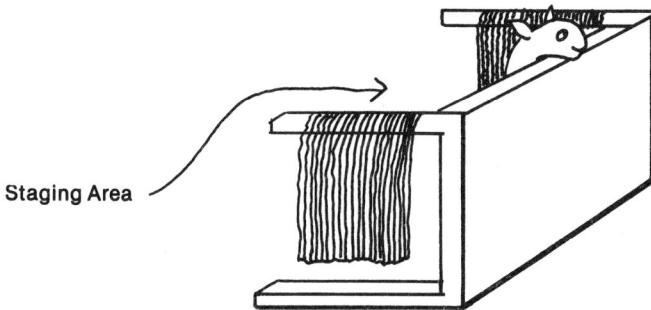

Staging Area

Follow-up: Demonstrate to the children how to get behind the card table and hold a puppet up over the edge of the table so viewers in front of the card table can see the puppet. Allow children to "try out" their new stage. The card table and towels fold for easy storage.

24

Individual
Small Group
Large Group *

Title: FLANNELBOARD

Purpose: To reinforce language development through story-telling with visual stimulation.

Materials Needed: Flannelboard
                                    Scissors
                                    Flannel scraps
                                    Children's story

Procedure:

The purpose of using visual aids to reinforce language development is to utilize more than just the auditory modality.

Very often the use of flannelboard visuals is made too difficult because the flannel characters are used much too extensively. It is suggested that flannel cutouts be held to a bare minimum.

For example, to tell *The Three Billy Goats Gruff*, you need only (1) a bridge, (2) a troll, and (3) a goat. The flannel goat can be used to illustrate each of the three billy goats.

Follow-up: Read *The Three Billy Goats Gruff* to your children, using flannel visuals to reinforce the story. Many good stories for children are available in Volume 2 of *Childcraft—the How & Why Library*, 1976. Field Enterprises Educational Corp., 510 Merchandise Mart Plaza, Chicago, IL 60654.

Title: **FINGER PUPPETS**

Purpose: To provide visual aid for story telling.

Materials Needed: Strips of paper, 2" x 5", 4
                          Box of crayons
                          Cellophane tape
                          Story—*The Three Billy Goats Gruff*
                          Glue
                          Paper scraps

Procedure:

The story of *The Three Billy Goats Gruff* can be reinforced visually by making four finger puppets to represent the three billy goats and the troll.

To make a finger puppet, wrap a 2" x 5" strip of paper around your finger and tape it into a cylinder. Decorate the cylinder to represent a story character (see sample below). Make 3 more cylinders and decorate them to represent the 3 billy goats and the troll.

The story of the three billy goats is used here only to illustrate how finger puppets add to a story. You may make the puppets to visually assist almost any children's story. Generally, all you need to do is to make cylinders for the main characters and hold each character up as his lines are delivered.

Follow-up: As a worthwhile art activity, have the children make their own finger puppets.

Billy Goat
Cylinder

26

Individual
Small Group   *
Large Group   *

Title: **PICTURES**

Purpose: To provide visual aid for story telling.

Materials Needed: Art paper, 5 pieces
                             Crayons or colored chalk

Procedure:

The story of *The Breman Town Musicians* is used here to illustrate how effectively the use of simple pictures can be used to supplement a story. The story of the "Musicians" relates the adventures of a donkey, dog, cat, and rooster and their final encounter with some robbers. To use visuals, make separate, simple pictures of the four animals and one of several robbers. As the story progresses, show the pictures of each of the characters as they are involved in the story.

Follow-up: Use the pictures to encourage the children to tell the story (or parts of it) in their own words.

Title: **MOBILES**

Purpose: To stimulate interest in language.

Materials Needed: Clothes hangers, 7
                          String, about 8' long or paper clips
                          File cards, 5" x 7", 11
                          Crayons
                          Poem—"The House that Jack Built"

Procedure:

The poem "The House that Jack Built" is used here to illustrate how a mobile can be used to enhance a poem or story.

First prepare the 5" x 7" cards with pictures of the objects and characters of the poem as suggested below. The pictures should depict: malt stalks, house, cat, rat, dog, cow, maiden, man, priest, cock, farmer.

Tie the hangers together and tie the 5" x 7" cards to the hangers. (If slight adjustments are necessary to acquire balance, you could attach paper clips to the hangers.)

Follow-up: Read (and re-read) the poem "The House that Jack Built" always using the mobile as a visual aid. You may point to the pictures or have the children point to the pictures.

Suggested
Hanger
Arrangement

Title: **SOCK PUPPETS**

Purpose: To stimulate interest in language activities.

Materials Needed: Cotton stocking
                       Pipe cleaners
                       Art paper scraps
                       Glue

Procedure:

Make a "book worm" puppet out of a cotton stocking. Insert your hand all the way into the stocking. Tuck the toe of the stocking between the thumb and the fingers to form the "worm's" mouth. Decorate the worm to your own satisfaction. Some suggestions are: eye glasses (can be made with pipe cleaners), beret, necktie, eyes, ears, tongue, and so on.

Use the worm as a friend who helps you hold the book when you are reading a storybook to the children.

Follow-up: Collect the necessary materials and let the children make their own sock puppets.

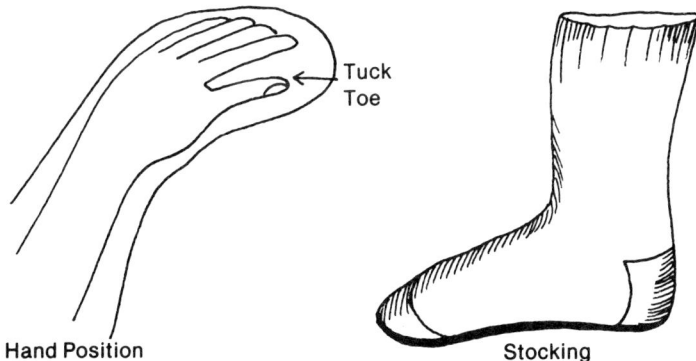

Tuck
Toe

Hand Position   Stocking

Title: **CEREAL BOX PUPPETS MADE BY TEACHER**

Purpose: To provide visual interest in stories.

Materials Needed: Cereal boxes, 2
Crayons
Scissors
Glue
Art paper scraps
Construction paper, 2 sheets
Story (*The Hare and the Tortoise* is
used here as an example.)

Procedure:

Prepare pictures of the hare and the tortoise as illustrated below. Next, prepare yourself to tell the story of *The Hare and the Tortoise.* Do not memorize the story, but know it well enough to tell it sequentially.

Cover the empty cereal boxes with construction paper, leaving the tops uncovered. Turn over the boxes and paste on cut-outs of the story characters.

Insert your hands into the boxes. As each character's lines are delivered, hold up the appropriate cereal box.

Follow-up: Have the children bring cereal boxes from home. When you have enough boxes, distribute art paper scraps, glue, scissors, material scraps, and so on. Have the children design and make their own cereal box puppets.

Cover with
Construction Paper

30

Title: **CEREAL BOX PUPPETS MADE BY CHILDREN**

Purpose: To stimulate conversation among children.

Materials Needed: Cereal boxes, 1 per child
Paste
Scissors
Paper scraps
Felt-tip markers
Yarn
Material scraps

Procedure:

Instruct the children to place their cereal boxes on their desks so that the top will be the bottom of the puppet. Then demonstrate many different ways the children can use material scraps, paste, and so on, to create faces for the puppets. Demonstrate how to punch a hole for the puppet's nose. Some children may need help with the nose hole. Place your hand inside the cereal box and put a finger through the nose hole.

Follow-up: Gather the children around for a story. Use your puppet to help tell the story.

Title: **STICK PUPPETS**

Purpose: To promote children's participation in language
       activities.

Materials Needed: Crayons
                       Art paper scraps
                       Glue
                       Scissors
                       Sticks (such as tongue depressors), 1 per
                          child
                       Story—*The Shepherd Boy and the Wolf*
                          by Aesop, *Childcraft*

Procedure:

Direct the children through the steps in making a wolf's
head as illustrated below. Then have the children cut out
their wolves' heads and glue them to their sticks (see below).

Next, gather the children around you for a story. Read
them the story of *The Shepherd Boy and the Wolf.* Discuss
the story and the moral connected to the story. Re-read the
story and instruct the children to listen for the lines, "Wolf,
wolf" and join in with you saying "Wolf, wolf" and at the
same time raise their sticks with the wolves' heads.

Follow-up: If your children are mature enough to grasp the
morals presented in fables, continue with others: "The Dove
and the Ant," "The Lion and the Mouse," "The Crow and
the Pitcher."

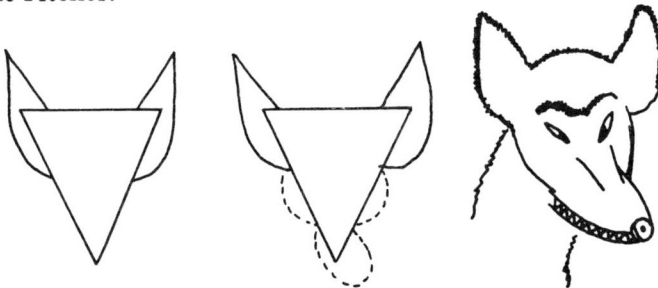

Title: PAPER PLATE PUPPETS

Purpose: To stimulate interest in books and stories.

Materials Needed: Paper plates, 2
Scissors
Green Crayon
Black Crayon
Stapler
Story—*The Clever Frog, Childcraft*

Procedure:

The story of "The Clever Frog" is adapted from an African folktale. The story relates a young man, Nzua, trying to get a written message asking to marry the Lord Sun's daughter. Nzua tries to get his animal friends to deliver the message to the Lord Sun's house in the sky. None can help. Then the frog says he can deliver the message.

With the help of a paper plate puppet, designed to look like a frog, read this four-page story to your children.

To make a paper plate frog, place one plate on top of the other, bend in half and then unfold. Staple the edges of the two plates together half way around (Figure 1). Also, cut two semicircles through the top plate only, along the fold as shown in Figure 2. Next, fold the semicircle up. Place hand inside to operate. The front view is shown in Figure 3. Decorate with crayons.

Follow-up: Provide two plates for each child. Staple half way around the edge. With crayons let the children create their own puppets.

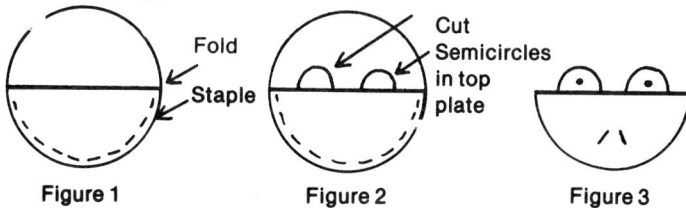

Figure 1   Figure 2   Figure 3

33

Title: OVERHEAD PROJECTOR

Purpose: To create interest in books and stories.

Materials Needed: Overhead projector
Construction paper, 2 pieces
Scissors
Story—*The Little Red Hen and the Grain of Wheat*

Procedure:

Prepare silhouettes of a hen, duck, cat, and dog by cutting out the outlines from half sheets of construction paper. Suggested outlines are provided below.

Gather the children into an area where they can all see the projection from the overhead projector. Read to the children the story of the *Little Red Hen.* As each character's lines are read, place the outline of that animal on the overhead projector and project the silhouette on the wall or screen. The story has repetitious segments the children will enjoy even more with the visual aids.

Follow-up: Prepare other silhouettes for a variety of stories.

Title: STOCKING HANGER PUPPET

Purpose: To stimulate interest in stories and books.

Materials Needed: Crayons
Wire clothes hanger
Nylon stocking (hose)
Art paper scraps
Glue
Scissors
Story—"The Lion and the Mouse" by
Aesop

Procedure:

Bend a hanger as illustrated below, and stretch a stocking over the hanger. Next, prepare the lion and the mouse from art paper and crayons. Glue the lion to one side of the hanger and the mouse to the other side.

Gather the children around you in a story-telling area. Read to the children the fable "The Lion and the Mouse." When the story refers to the lion, show the children the lion side of the puppet. Turn the puppet to the mouse side when referring to the mouse.

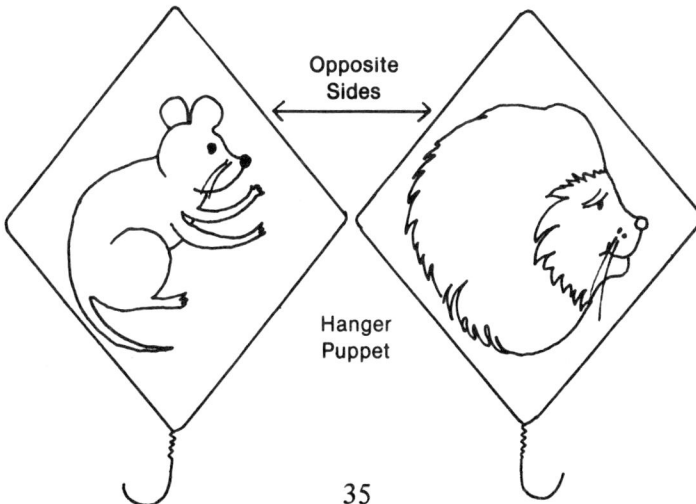

Opposite Sides

Hanger Puppet

35

Follow-up: Make additional puppets for additional stories. The puppets store easily by hanging them on a hanger rod in a coat closet. Over a few years you can amass a sizeable collection of hanger puppets.

Individual
Small Group *
Large Group *

Title: **USING SLIDES OF CLASSIC PAINTINGS**

Purpose: To stimulate language usage.

Materials Needed: Slide projector
2" x 2" slides of classic paintings
(To illustrate how to use a slide to inspire discussion, the slide of "Whistler's Mother" is used here.)

Procedure:

Visit your public library. Many libraries have slides of famous paintings that can be checked out. If available, check out the slide of "Whistler's Mother." This picture portrays the image of an elderly woman, sitting passively in a rocking chair. Her hands are folded, eyes lowered. Beside the woman is a small table on which there are a book and a small lamp.

Project the slide on a wall and allow plenty of time for children to view the image.

Some suggested questions to initiate discussion are: "Why do you think the woman is sad?" or "What do you think the woman is thinking about?"

When asked why the woman was sad, one five-year-old boy said, "I don't think she's sad. I think she just finished the book and she's thinking about the ending."

Conversation usually becomes spontaneous as the children view the slides.

Note: Be sure to mention the titles and artists as you view the slides. After all, the children are studying famous paintings.

36

Title: **MAKING VISUAL AIDS**

Purpose: Using free and inexpensive materials to make visual aids.

Materials Needed: Round oatmeal boxes
Empty bleach jugs
Bathroom tissue cores
Paper
Etc.

Procedure:

The suggestions for making "visuals" in this unit include many kinds of materials. Nearly all of those suggested visuals could be substituted by using cylindrical materials such as tissue cores and round containers.

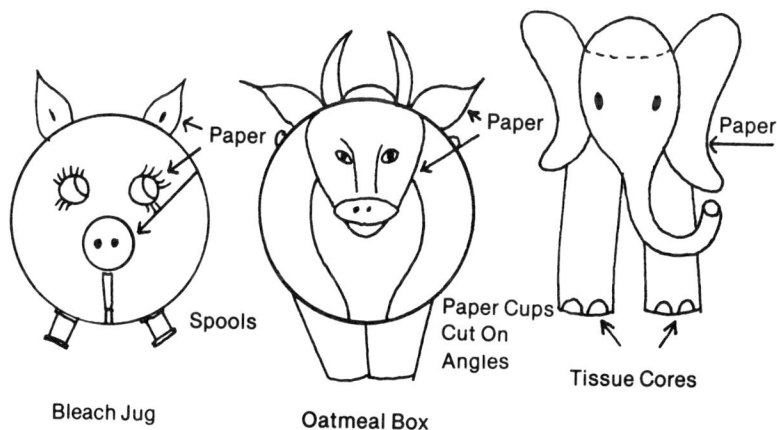

Bleach Jug   Oatmeal Box

37

Title: **NO MORE WIGGLES**

Purpose: To provide a meaningful opening for quiet activities.

Materials Needed: None

Procedure:

At the beginning of the day or during transition from an active period to a passive period, gather the children around in a circle, sitting on the floor. Then, teach them the following poem:

> I wiggle my fingers (wiggle hands)
> I wiggle my toes (wiggle feet)
> I wiggle my shoulders (shake shoulders)
> I wiggle my nose (wrinkle nose)
> Now no more wiggles are left in me
> So I will be still, as still can be.
>   (Fold hands in lap)

Follow-up: Be prepared to go directly into next activity (story time, sharing time, and so on). If there is a time lag, children will become restless.

Title: THERE WAS A CROOKED WITCH

Purpose: To provide a language activity during Halloween time.

Materials Needed: None

Procedure:

During a passive period, have the children sit in a circle. Then, with flare and dramatics, tell the following poem:

I saw a crooked witch flying through the sky,
With a little crooked smile and a twinkle in her eye.
She had a skinny crooked nose,
That pointed downward to her toes.
She wore a tall and crooked hat,
And carried a black and crooked cat.
She scared me so, I had to run,
Isn't Halloween fun!!

Follow-up: With the assistance of the children, prepare a bulletin board or mobile that illustrates the poem.

Individual　*
Small Group　*
Large Group　*

Title:　　SHORT STORIES FOR CHILDREN

Purpose: To extend the attention of children by providing heavy exposure to short stories.

Materials Needed:　Collection of short stories

Procedure:

Provide a regular time slot in the curriculum for reading stories to children. There are many benefits derived from reading stories to children including vocabulary development, concept clarification, interest in books, and an extension of the attention span. Short stories are especially helpful for developing attention spans and are readily available in popular journals.

Journals that frequently publish excellent short stories for children are: *Instructor, Family Circle, Teacher, Highlights for Children, Early Years.*

Check the *back issues* of these journals for your collection of short stories.

Follow-up: The next time you're in your library check on some of the following short Christmas stories: "Mrs. Angie and the Christmas Rose" (*Instructor*, Dec. 1959), "The Year Santa Went Modern" (*Family Circle*, Dec. 1963), "The Christmas Star" (*Instructor*, Dec. 1958), "Kathie's Christmas Present" (*Instructor*, Dec. 1962), "Mummer's Secret" (*Instructor*, Dec. 1962), "The Best Present" (*Highlights for Children*, Dec. 1958), "A Whale of a Christmas" (*Highlights for Children*, Dec. 1958), "Santa's Longies" (*Instructor*, Dec. 1967), "Reindeer Mystery" (*Instructor*, Dec. 1958), "The Mole Family's Christmas" (*Family Circle*, Dec. 1969), "Gift from the Past" (*Instructor*, Dec. 1969), "A Small Miracle" (*Instructor*, Dec. 1963), "The Christmas Santa Almost Missed" (*Family Circle*, Dec. 1968).

Individual   *
Small Group *
Large Group *

Title: **SEQUENCING STORIES**

Purpose: To develop meaningful sequence of events.

Materials Needed: Storybook
Pictures that depict major points of the
story

Procedure:

Gather the children in an area where they can sit in a circle
or semicircle near you. Tell or read the selected story to the
children. Use a bit of flare and dramatics when relating the
story. Use the pictures to illustrate the major points of the
story. As the pictures are presented, place them in view of
the children in the proper story-related sequence.

Follow-up: When the children know the story well enough
to tell it, let them practice placing the pictures in proper
sequence while telling the story.

Individual   *
Small Group *
Large Group *

Title: **READING FOR KNOWLEDGE**

Purpose: To transfer knowledge to children.

Materials Needed: A book designed to be informational

Procedure:

Gather the children into a comfortable setting. It's important for the children to be seated with adequate space and ventilation.

Select a book that is informational in nature. There are numerous books of excellent quality that relate information or values that you can use for discussion topics leading to understanding.

Suggested books about human characteristics: *What Happened to George?* (fat) by Betty Englebretson, *The Smallest Boy in the Class* by J. Bien, *Rosa-Too-Little* by Sue Felt, *Finders Keepers* (greed) by William Riokind, *Palle's New Suit* (responsibility) by Elza Beskow, *Papa Small* (relationships) by Lois Lenski. Suggested books about various races and cultures: *Hat for a Hero* (Mexican) by L. Bannon, *Two Is a Team* (Black) by L. Beim, *Madeline's Rescue* (French) by L. Bemelmans, *Lonesome Boy* (Black) by A. Bontemps, *Story About Ping* (Chinese) by M. Flack, *Dee Bee's Birthday* (Chinese) by Y. Liang, *Faraway Holiday* (Mexican) by Eula Long, *Little Leo* (Italian) by Leo Politi, *Hello Henry* (Black) by E. Vogel, *Red Fox and His Canoe* (Indian) by N. Benchley, *Timinoto's Great Adventure* (Japanese) by F. Francis.

Follow-up: After an informational story, hold a group discussion to review and clarify concepts presented in the story.

Concepts developed in the stories can frequently be transferred to your class and/or community. These are the bases for social studies in early childhood education.

Title: **CLASSIC TALES**

Purpose: To acquaint children with classic children's stories.

Materials Needed: A classic storybook

Procedure:

Gather the children into a comfortable setting. It's important for the children to be seated with adequate space and ventilation.

Read to the children one of the truly classic children's stories. Be sure to have it pre-read and be sure to share illustrations and other prepared visual aids with the children.

Some suggested classics are: *Pinocchio, Bambi, Peter Pan, Alice in Wonderland, Peter Rabbit, Brer Rabbit, The Twelve Days of Christmas, Rudolph the Red Nose Reindeer, Little Drummer Boy, Jack and the Beanstalk, Snow White.*

Follow-up: Remember that classic children's literature is meant to be enjoyed. There need be no other reason for using valuable school time for enjoying it. Set a story time priority for you and your classroom children and keep it.

Title: **TELLING STORIES**

Purpose: To develop a fondness for language and stories.

Materials Needed: Knowledge of a good story

                           Visual aids to support the story

Procedure:

Read the story over and over until you can tell the story without memorizing it. Prepare visual aids to support the story. (For visual aid suggestions, see pages 24-37 in this book.)

Gather the children around you in a semicircle. Present the story in an enthusiastic manner, but don't dramatize to the point that it detracts from the story.

Suggestions: Stories the children will enjoy are too numerous to list. A few suggestions are: *The Three Bears, The Three Little Pigs, Billy Goats Gruff, Little Red Riding Hood, Where the Wild Things Are, Hailstones and Halibut Bones.* For further suggestions see the bibliographies near the back of this book.

Individual   *
Small Group *
Large Group *

Title: **CREATIVE STORY TELLING**

Purpose: To develop creative language usage.

Materials Needed: None

Procedure:

Develop the knack of creating short, exciting stories that children can hear once or twice and know well enough to repeat.

Developing these short stories is not difficult if you can create a catchy title that in itself relates much of the story. For example "The Cat That Chased Dogs." This title relates the story. All you need to do is pick the setting (familiar to the children), pick the story characters (usually children 5 to 8 years old), and develop the story line. Other titles that set the stage for short story time are "The Giant Pizza," "The Runaway Skateboard," "The Magic Roller Skates," "The Birthday Secret."

Gather the children about you in a semicircle. Tell a short, creative story. Then, lead the children in a discussion of the story. Ask "creative questions," such as, "What do you suppose would happen if . . .?" or "Why do you think . . .?"

Follow-up: Prepare a bulletin board that has four pictures about your story. The four pictures should illustrate (1) the beginning of the story, (2) the action, (3) the climax, and (4) the ending.

Using the four pictures as visual aids, ask individual children to tell the story.

45

Title: MY PICTURE WORD BOOK—OPPOSITES

Purpose: To develop the concept of opposites.

Materials Needed: Old magazine supply
                       Scissors, 1 pair per child
                       Glue
                       Hole punch
                       Yarn, approximately 12" long per child
                       Construction paper, 9" x 12", 2 sheets
                           per child

Procedure:

Cut the construction paper into quarters and distribute eight sheets, 4½" x 6", to each child. Punch two holes along the left margin and bind the eight sheets with yarn. Each child now has a booklet with fourteen interior pages.

Hold a series of discussions with your children explaining the meaning of word opposites. Use whatever classroom props available to assist in the series of discussions. These discussions should be held over a period of days or weeks.

Suggested word opposites to teach the children are: in-out, big-little, short-tall, light-dark, front-back, wet-dry, hot-cold.

Follow-up: Distribute magazines, glue, and scissors to the children. Help them find pictures that depict the word opposites suggested above. Direct the children to glue the word opposite pictures on facing pairs of pages in their booklets.

On the cover of the booklets, print MY WORD BOOK: OPPOSITES. Use booklets to remind the children of the word opposites. Later, request parents to use the booklets at home to reinforce vocabulary.

Title: MY PICTURE WORD BOOK–SPACE

Purpose: To develop vocabulary related to spatial relationships.

Materials Needed: Stars, gummed
                      Old magazine supply
                      Scissors, 1 pair per child
                      Glue
                      Hole punch
                      Yarn, approximately 12" long per child
                      Construction paper, 9" x 12", 2 sheets
                          per child

Procedure:

Cut the construction paper into quarters and distribute
eights sheets, 4½" x 6", to each child. Punch two holes along
the left margin and bind the eight sheets with yarn.

Hold a series of discussions with your children explaining
the meaning of spatial words. Use whatever classroom props
you need to assist in the explanation. These discussions
should be held over a period of days or weeks.

Suggested words to introduce are: top, over, above, up,
on, high, front, behind, under, underneath, below, down,
beside.

Distribute the scissors, magazines, and glue to the children. Direct them to cut out and glue pictures of persons or
things on the fourteen inside pages of their booklets.

On the cover of the booklets, print MY WORD BOOK–
SPACE.

With as much supervision from you as necessary, have the
children stick the gummed stars on the pages in spatial
relationship to the pictures, e.g., over, beside, under, and so
on.

Note: If the children are too young for such an

extended assignment, cut the project down by quartering only one sheet of paper which makes a booklet with just six interior pages.

Follow-up: Use the booklets' picture clues to remind children of the spatial vocabulary. See if the children can recall the vocabulary words by seeing the position of the stars in relationship to the pictures.

Title: MY PICTURE WORD BOOK–DATES AND RATES

Purpose: To develop vocabulary related to the abstract themes of time, relative time, and rate.

Materials Needed: Old magazine supply
Scissors, 1 pair per child
Glue
Hole punch
Yarn, approximately 12" long per child
Construction paper, 9" x 12", 2 sheets per child

Procedure:

Cut the construction paper into quarters and distribute eight sheets, 4½" x 6", to each child. Punch two holes along the left margin and bind the eight sheets with yarn. Each child now has a booklet with fourteen interior pages.

Hold a series of discussions with your children explaining the meaning of words that relate time and rate concepts. These terms are generally very *abstract.* If the children in your class are quite young, you should consider delaying the introduction of the more abstract concepts.

Suggested words for introduction to children are: slow, fast, early, late, first, last, day, and night. More difficult words to understand are: yesterday, today, tomorrow, day, week, month.

Follow-up: Distribute magazines, scissors, and glue to the children. Help them find pictures that depict the words suggested above. Only you can determine, through observation, which, if any, of the concepts are too difficult for the children. Direct the children to glue pictures depicting concepts they understand into their booklets.

On the cover of the booklet, print MY WORD BOOK– DATES AND RATES. Later, use the booklets to review the dates-rates vocabulary.

49

Individual   *
Small Group   *
Large Group   *

Title: MY PICTURE WORD BOOK—BODY LOCALIZATION

Purpose: To develop vocabulary related to body parts.

Materials Needed: Old magazine supply
Scissors, 1 pair per child
Glue
Hole punch
Yarn, approximately 12" long per child
Construction paper, 9" x 12", 2 sheets
per child

Procedure:

Cut the construction paper into quarters and distribute eight sheets, 4½" x 6", to each child. Punch two holes along the left margin and bind the eight sheets with yarn.

Hold a series of discussions with your children reinforcing the names of body parts. These discussions should be held over a period of days or weeks.

Suggested words to review with the children are: eyes, nose, mouth, ears, chin, hair, hands, fingers, elbows, arms, legs, knees, feet, ankles.

Follow-up: Distribute magazines, glue, and scissors to the children. Help them find pictures that depict the words related to body parts suggested above. Direct the children to glue the pictures, one per page, in their booklets.

On the cover of the booklets, print MY WORD BOOK—BODY PARTS. Use the booklets to review with children the names of body parts. Later, you can send the booklets home with the children along with a request for parents to assist their children with the words.

Individual   *
Small Group *
Large Group *

Title: **BULLETIN BOARD: LARGE OR SMALL,
BIG OR LITTLE**

Purpose: To develop vocabulary related to size.

Materials Needed: Bulletin board
Lettering
Pictures of large objects (cut from magazines)
Mounting paper, 10 half sheets
Glue
Yarn, 5 eight-inch lengths

Procedure:

Prepare a bulletin board presenting large and small pictures mounted on construction paper. Pair large and small pictures by pinning a length of yarn from pictures of large objects to pictures of small objects.

Suggested pictures are: elephant-kitten, truck-toy, tree-flower, airplane-bird, football player-baby, and so on.

Gather the children around you near the bulletin board. Discuss the meanings of large and small and explain how big and little have the same meanings as large and small. Point out the picture pairings on the bulletin board as you discuss the words.

Follow-up: During a sharing time, review the words and have selected children point out items in the room that illustrate the large-small, big-little concepts.

Title: **BULLETIN BOARD: ROUGH OR SMOOTH**

Purpose: To develop vocabulary related to texture.

Materials Needed: Bulletin board
Lettering
Rough material, 3 items
Smooth material, 3 items
Construction paper, 6 half sheets
Glue

Procedure:

Prepare a bulletin board presenting rough and smooth items mounted on half sheets of construction paper. Label the board with the word "rough" and "smooth." These words are intended for exposure, not a reading lesson.

Suggested items for mounting are: sandpaper, peanut shell, pine cones, wax paper, plastic spoon, fingernail file, marble, and so on.

Gather the children around you near the bulletin board. Discuss the meanings of rough and smooth. Have the children repeat the words. To reinforce the auditory stimulation, it is important for the children to *touch* rough and smooth surfaces.

Follow-up: Solicit additional rough and smooth items from the children's homes.

Title: PROMINENT PERSONALITIES:
              MARTIN LUTHER KING, JR.

Purpose: To provide opportunities to express ideas about prominent people using oral language.

Materials Needed: Pictures of Martin Luther King, Jr.
                      Story about Martin Luther King, Jr.
                      Tape recorder with tape

Procedure:

Mount the pictures of Dr. King in a prominent place. Question the children about the pictures. Ask them what they know about Dr. King. A day or two later read a story to the children about Dr. King. After the story is read, let the children, one at a time, tell what they know about Dr. King and simultaneously record their comments on tape.

Read short stories about many famous Americans for future class discussions: Lincoln, Washington, Carver, Babe Ruth, Daniel Boone, and so on.

Follow-up: At a later time, listen to the tapes. Discuss what was said and how the voices sounded on tape.

Title: **DRAMATIC PLAY**

Purpose: To utilize oral language.

Materials Needed: Props for a story (such as table, chairs, and mats for acting out *The Three Bears*)

Procedure:

Gather the children into an area with space for movement. Select a well-known story and review it with the children. Next, select children to portray the characters in the story and place the story props in place. For example, if *The Three Bears* is selected, place the table, chairs, and mats in place and cast the roles of the bears and Goldilocks. There are several options for relating the story. (1) You verbalize the entire story, the actors act out the story, spectators observe. (2) You narrate the story except for the direct lines, actors act out story and say lines ("Someone tasted my porridge and ate it all up"), spectators observe.

Follow-up: Rotate the cast of characters so all children who wish to participate have ample opportunity. If you feel some children are capable of narrating the story, provide the opportunity.

Individual
Small Group *
Large Group *

Title: SETTING THE SCENE FOR SPEAKING:
GUESSING PANTOMIME

Purpose: To promote oral language usage.

Materials Needed: None

Procedure:

Gather the children about you in a semicircle. Ask the children, "How many of you have jobs to do at home?" Then comment on how helpful children can be when they help their parents with work around the home.

Say, "Think of jobs around the house. Then, we will take turns acting out jobs while the rest of the group guesses what job you are pretending to do."

When the children are guessing the pantomime, you may wish to add to the discussion by inserting questions, such as, "Is Tommy enjoying this job?" or "How can you tell if this job requires muscle?" "Why is Jana being very careful and gentle?"

Follow-up: Pantomime quizzes may be extended from household chores to include games (baseball) or children's stories (*The Three Bears*).

55

Title: **SETTING THE SCENE FOR SPEAKING:
BLOCK CENTER**

Purpose: To promote oral language usage.

Materials Needed: Large set of blocks
Strips of scrap paneling (or suitable substitute)
Suggested sizes:

2" x 4" - 2 each
2" x 6" - 2 each
2" x 8" - 2 each
2" x 10" - 4 each
2" x 12" - 4 each

Procedure:

Place the blocks and strips strategically in the classroom so traffic patterns do not interfere with block building experiences.

From day to day, assign different children to free-play at the block center in order to assure all children opportunities to engage in this highly beneficial activity.

Playing in a block center offers many challenges to children. While exploring and creating with blocks, children communicate freely. Adding strips of paneling to the block set (strips of cardboard may be used) encourages children to create buildings that include spans and roofs.

Follow-up: Before children arrive at school, add some toy cars and/or trucks to the block center. When children arrive, observe how they incorporate props into the building scheme.

Try other props such as tin soldiers, trees, shrubbery, and so on.

Individual
Small Group *
Large Group

Title: SETTING THE SCENE FOR SPEAKING:
HOUSEKEEPING CENTER

Purpose: To promote oral language usage.

Materials Needed: Toy kitchen (stove, sink, table, chairs)
Toy dishes

Procedure:

Place the toy kitchen (child-sized) in a corner of the room where semi-privacy is likely. Have the housekeeping center available for casual, walk-up play during free-play time. Also, during planned work time, assign a small group of children to play in the center.

In this type setting, children will imitate adult roles and will converse in adult-like language.

Generally, one child will assume a dominant role and assign roles to other children. For example, one child might say, "I'll be the mother. I'm cooking breakfast. You be the father. Sit there. Here's your coffee. This doll will be Baby Jill," and so on.

Follow-up: From time to time, arrange for the more reserved children to play in the housekeeping center. If these shy children are reluctant, let them watch the housekeeping center a few times (reflective play) before actually participating (imitative play).

Individual
Small Group *
Large Group

Title: **SETTING THE SCENE FOR SPEAKING:**
DRESSING CORNER

Purpose: To promote oral language usage.

Materials Needed: Various dress-up costumes (described below)

Procedure:

Children participate freely in oral communication when allowed to dress up and role play various adult roles.

Suggested adult roles and dress-up kits are:

(a) *Fireman.* Plastic fireman's hat, hose, cardboard box converted into fire truck.

(b) *Nurse.* White cap, kit, elastic bandage, old or toy stethescope, band-aids.

(c) *Carpenter.* Toy tool kit, nail apron, light lumber, bench, cap.

(d) *Teacher.* Small chalk board, chalk, eraser, books, desk.

(e) *Grocer.* Money tokens, toy or simulated groceries, toy counter (box), toy cash register (box).

Follow-up: You can stimulate thinking by asking children productive questions that they can answer by acting out the response in a dress-up setting. For example, say, "Pam, you pretend you had a bad fall on the sidewalk. Lisa, show us how you think the nurse would take care of Pam."

Individual
Small Group   *
Large Group

Title: **SPEAKING IN SENTENCES: TELEPHONE**

Purpose: To practice speaking in complete sentences.

Materials Needed: None

Procedure:

Join the children sitting in a circle on the floor. You start the "telephone message" by whispering a complete sentence (simple or compound) into the ear of the child on your left. Direct the children to keep the message going around the circle by way of whispers. By the time the message travels around the circle to the child on your right, it will probably be somewhat distorted. Ask the last child (on your right) to tell the other children what the message was when he/she received it. Then you tell them what it was when you started it.

Follow-up: Let some of the children start the message. Remind them to speak in complete sentences.

Sample Sentence: One day the hen was scratching in the barnyard when she found a grain of wheat.

Individual
Small Group   *
Large Group

Title: **SPEAKING IN SENTENCES: NO PEEK QUIZ**

Purpose: To practice speaking in complete sentences.

Materials Needed: Classroom objects: paper clip, chalk, chalk eraser, ball-point pen
                       Blindfold

Procedure:

Join the children sitting in a circle on the floor. Select one

59

child to be "it." He/She stands in the middle of the circle with the blindfold shielding his/her vision. Have the child cup his/her hands in preparation for receiving one of the classroom objects. Next, place one of the objects in the child's hands. The child is then supposed to identify the object via touch. He/She says "The object in my hands is a *paper clip*" or "The object in my hands is a *ball-point pen*," but always identify the object through speaking in complete sentences.

(If necessary, discuss the names of the classroom objects with the children before the game begins.)

Follow-up: If a child successfully identifies all the objects and correctly speaks in complete sentences, he is a winner. The game can have many winners.

Individual
Small Group *
Large Group

Title: **SPEAKING IN SENTENCES: PANTOMIME QUIZ**

Purpose: To practice speaking in complete sentences.

Materials Needed: None

Procedure:

Join the children sitting in a circle on the floor. Select one child to be "it." The "it" child stands in the middle of the circle and acts out an activity such as: washing hair, rowing a boat, fishing, setting the table, playing ping-pong, giving the dog a bath, and so on. The children in the circle observe the pantomime. If a child thinks he/she knows the answer, he/she raises his/her hand. You call on the child who then responds in a complete sentence, "Bobby is acting like he is *swimming*," or "Janet is acting like she is *setting the table*." If the answer is correct and stated in a complete sentence, that child gets to be "it."

Follow-up: Remind the children to speak in complete sentences during day-to-day activities.

60

Title: **SPEAKING IN SENTENCES:
WALKING AND SEEING**

Purpose: To practice speaking in complete sentences.

Materials Needed: None

Procedure:

Prepare the children to take a neighborhood walk by re-
viewing the rules of safety and good conduct. Also, clue the
children that the walk is especially for *seeing* many different
things. Prepare them for the discussion following the walk by
telling them, "When we get back from our walk, we are going
to share what we *saw.* Remember how we learned to talk in
complete sentences? We are going to discuss and share our
walk by talking in complete sentences."

Upon returning from the walk, join the children sitting
in a circle on the floor. Start the discussion by saying, "On
our walk I saw a robin on the ground." Starting to the left
and in turn around the circle, give each child a chance to say
a complete sentence.

Follow-up: Each morning, thereafter, remind the children
to speak in complete sentences.

Title: **SPEAKING IN SENTENCES:**
                  WALKING AND HEARING

Purpose: To practice speaking in complete sentences.

Materials Needed: None

Procedure:

Prepare the children to take a neighborhood walk by re-
viewing the rules of safety and good conduct. Also, clue the
children that the walk is especially for *hearing* many different
things. Prepare them for the discussion following the walk by
saying, "When we get back from our walk, we are going to
share what we *heard*. We are going to discuss and share our
walk by talking in complete sentences."

Upon returning from the walk, join the children sitting in
a circle on the floor. Start the discussion by saying, "On our
walk I heard a train whistle." Starting to the left and in turn
around the circle, give each child a chance to say a complete
sentence.

Follow-up: Be a good model by using complete sentences in
classroom activities.

Title: **THE HUMMING SOUNDS—M AND N**

Purpose: To reinforce the recognition of letters.

Materials Needed: Construction paper, 9" x 12", 2 sheets
per child
Scissors, 1 pair per child
Glue
Old magazines and newspapers
Stapler

Procedure:

When teaching letters, introduce the humming sounds first. Help the children search through magazines and newspapers to find and cut out pictures that start with M and N and to find and cut out the letters M and N.

On one piece of art paper, have the children glue their M letters and pictures, and on the other page, glue their N letters and pictures.

When both pages are finished, place them face to face and staple them along the left edge.

On the front, print MY M and N BOOKLET.

Follow-up: Send the booklets home with the children so they can use the booklets with their parents.

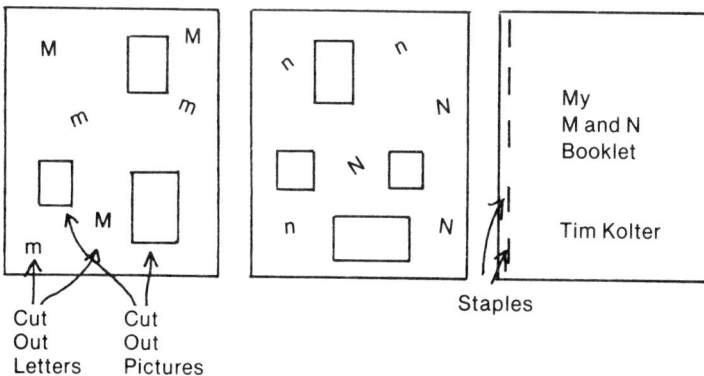

63

Individual   *
Small Group *
Large Group *

Title: **THE EXPLOSIVE SOUNDS–B, T, P, D**

Purpose: To reinforce the recognition of letters.

Materials Needed: Construction paper, 9" x 12", 3 sheets
per child
Scissors, 1 pair per child
Glue
Old magazines and newspapers
Stapler

*Procedure:*ʼ

When teaching letter recognition, introduce the humming
sounds M and N first followed by the explosive sounds – B,
D, P, T.

Over a period of several days have the children search
through magazines and newspapers for pictures starting with
the explosive sounds and the actual letters B, D, P, and T.
You will have to do most of the identifying, but the children
can do the cutting. On the first sheet of paper, have the
children glue the "B" pictures and letters, on the second
sheet have them glue the "T" pictures and letters. *Now,* turn
the "T" page over and *on the other side,* have the children
glue the "P" pictures and letters. On the third sheet have the
children glue the "D" pictures and letters. The letters and
pictures should be glued randomly. (See previous activity
entitled "The Humming Sounds – M and N") Place the
finished pages so the B and T are face-to-face and the P and
D are face-to-face. Staple down along the left edge of the
cover. On the cover print MY B, T, P, and D BOOKLET.

Follow-up: Send the booklets home with the children so
they can use the booklets with their parents.

Title: **TEACHING LOWERCASE LETTERS**

Purpose: To provide a model of lowercase letters.

Materials Needed: Primary pencils
                          Printscript paper

Procedure:

Use the lowercase letters provided here as models for printscript. You may wish to make some variations. Note that the t and d are slightly shorter than other "tall" letters. Once you have introduced the letters, make every effort to be consistent.

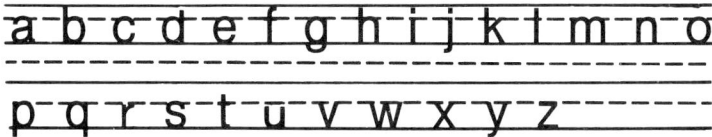

a b c d e f g h i j k l m n o
p q r s t u v w x y z

Follow-up: Send a sample of all lowercase letters home with the children so parental assistance can be consistent with school instruction.

Title: **TEACHING CAPITAL LETTERS**

Purpose: To provide a model of uppercase letters.

Materials Needed: Primary pencils
                          Printscript paper

Procedure:

Use the capital letters provided here as models for print-script. Before you introduce the capitals, you may wish to make some variations on some letters which tend to be different from area to area. Consistency is the most important aspect of printscript.

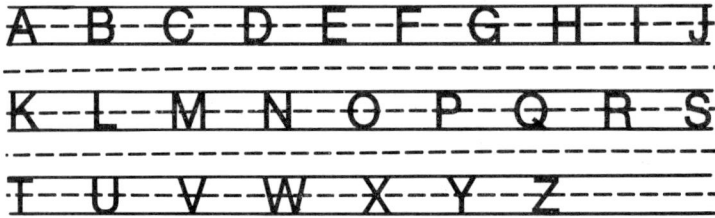

A B C D E F G H I J

K L M N O P Q R S

T U V W X Y Z

Follow-up: Send a sample of all uppercase and lowercase letters home with the children so parental assistance can be consistent with school instruction.

Individual   *
Small Group   *
Large Group   *

Title: **WRITING NAMES IN PRINTSCRIPT**

Purpose: To demonstrate proper use of uppercase and lowercase.

Materials Needed: Primary pencils, 1 per child
Printscript paper

Procedure:

In advance, print each child's name individually on a piece of printscript paper. Distribute the papers to the children. Be sure the children are holding their pencils properly with their papers placed at proper angles.

Have the children trace their names several times before printing without guides. Most children will have some experience with writing their names. Be sure to emphasize that names (generally) start with a capital letter and the rest of the letters are lowercase.

Janet

Follow-up: Send a sample of correct printscript, as shown here, home with the children. Well-meaning parents sometimes teach their children to print their names entirely in capital letters.

66

Individual   *
Small Group *
Large Group *

Title: **LETTER PUZZLES: MATCHING**

Purpose: To promote an understanding of letter names and letter sounds.

Materials Needed: Construction paper, 9" x 12", 1 per child
                       Pictures cut from magazines
                       Paste
                       Paper punch
                       Yarn, 12" long, 4 or 5 per child
                       Felt-tip pen

Procedure:

Direct each child to select four or five pictures to paste on the right side of the paper. Then help each child decide which letters represent the beginning sounds of the pictures already pasted on each paper. Help each child print the letters on the left side of his paper, but in a scrambled order. Punch a hole beside each letter and each picture. Help the children tie a 12" piece of yarn in each hole next to each letter. Then, show the children how to thread the yarn through the hole next to the picture that corresponds with the letter of its beginning sound.

Follow-up: Have the children swap their "Letter Puzzles" with other children so they can practice many different sounds.

Title: **JIGSAW PUZZLES**

Purpose: To promote children's understanding of uppercase and lowercase letters.

Materials Needed: File cards, 5" x 7", 26
Felt-tip pen
Scissors

Procedure:

Print each letter of the alphabet in uppercase and lowercase on a 5" x 7" file card as shown below, and make a set of 26 puzzles by cutting the cards in two on a random line between the two letters. On the back side of the letter pieces, number the puzzles so they can be easily matched and stored by children. For example, on each half of the back side of the letter A, number 1; on each back half of the B, number 2; on each back half of the C, number 3; and so on.

If available, laminate the puzzle pieces.

Follow-up: Make the puzzles available for children to use at playtime. Encourage parents to make a set of puzzles for home use.

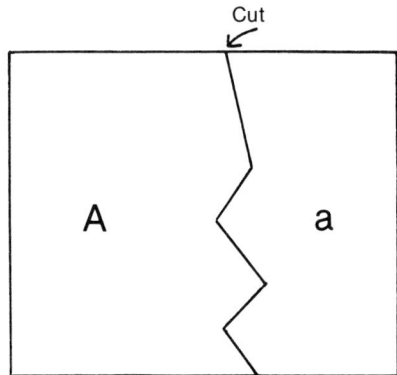

Cut

A   a

Title: **BEGINNING CONSONANTS
USING THE MATHULATOR**

Purpose: To provide self-checking consonant activities.

Materials Needed: Shoe box
File cards, 3" x 5", 20
Scissors
Glue
Magazine supply
Felt-tip pen

Procedure:

The mathulator is a teacher-made device originally designed as a self-checking activity for number readiness. It is also described in the Number Readiness Activities unit of this series.

Cut a 3" x 1¼" slot in the top of a shoe box as shown in Figure 1. In the end of the box, the one furthest from the slot in the top, cut a ¾" diameter hole, Figure 2. The shoe box mathulator is now ready for use.

Next, prepare about twenty 3" x 5" cards for use in the mathulator. First, cut the cards into the shape of a T as

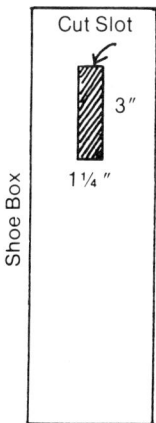

Figure 1
Top View

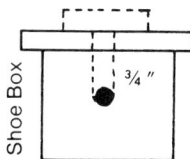

Figure 2
End View

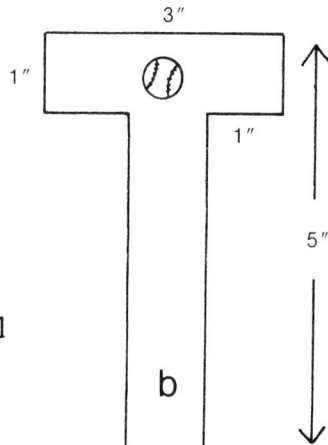

Figure 3

shown in Figure 3. From magazines, cut the pictures of objects starting with the consonants you are currently teaching the children. Glue the picture in the middle of the crossbar of the T. Near the bottom of the stem of the T, print the consonant. Place the twenty T's in the slot of the mathulator (Figure 2). The child looks at the picture on the T and states the beginning consonant. He/She can then look through the hole to check his/her work.

Follow-up: You may use the mathulator for a wide range of language arts and beginning reading activities. In addition to beginning consonants, some other suggestions are: ending consonants, medial vowel sounds, long vowel sounds, blends, and sight words.

Ending Consonants   Medial Vowels   Long Vowels

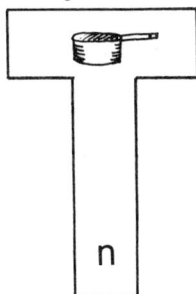

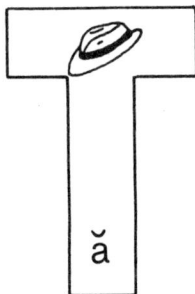

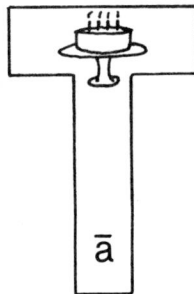

Sight Words   Blends

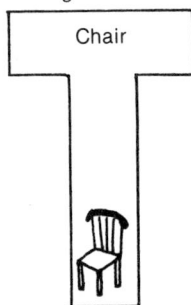

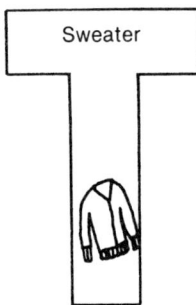

FOR THE TEACHER

This section provides a number of useful resources for planning and presenting language development activities for young children.

Title: **THE A.B.C'S OF SELECTING AND USING CHILDREN'S LITERATURE IN EARLY CHILDHOOD EDUCATION***

*A*uthors and illustrators serve as cues to quality and type of book; learn which are the most talented and prolific.

*B*ig books are not always the best books. There is little correlation between size and quality.

*C*lassifications are important; they enable you to find the right book at the right time.

*D*on't judge a book by its cover—or title—or age.

*E*njoy the book, if you want the children to do likewise.

*F*ind the best book to "fill the bill." With so many good books, you can be selective.

*G*ood books are worth remembering, but don't trust memory; keep a card file or list.

*H*old the book so all children can see it when you are reading to a group. Learn to read upside down or sideways, if necessary.

*I*nclude children in story-time activities. They love to help read or tell a story!

*J*udge a book on the basis of its value to you and your current class; tastes differ.

*K*indergarten is the place where children learn to like *or* dislike reading. You have a great responsibility to nurture a love of reading and learning.

*L*ibraries and library corners should be utilized to give children access to many books.

*M*ake books available by giving *time* for children to view, handle, and study a good selection.

*N*ever continue the reading or telling of a story beyond the interest level of children.

*O*bserve children's reactions to literature. They are honest and realistic critics.

*These guidelines for selecting and using children's literature were developed by Ruby Gaston and are used with permission.

*P*rime the pump. Use your ingenuity to develop interest and curiosity in advance.

*Q*uiet cooperation should be expected of your listening audience. But don't demand sitting at rigid attention on stiff, hard seats.

*R*ead at the level of your group. Work toward more complex books during the school year.

*S*peed of reading should be determined by such factors as children's interest, pace of story, and difficulty of text.

*T*ime the presentation of a story; find the best time of the *year* and *day* for a story.

*U*nit, subject or seasonal topics can usually serve as guides to wise selection of books.

*V*ary the types of books throughout the school year. Variety is the spice of literature.

*W*atch your grammar, diction, tone, volume, and pronunciation for good presentation.

E*x*amine the books, stories and poems in advance to familiarize yourself with key factors, dialogue, expressive phrases, and overall progression.

*Y*ou determine the success of children's literature. Pick wisely and present interestingly!

*Z*ealousness on the part of the reader or storyteller pays enormous dividends. Project the story and your enthusiasm to make story-time a great time!

Title: **STORY HELPS**

Examples of how to animate and illustrate children's stories:

Flannel-graph

Puppets

Sketch

Build-up procedure

Pantomime for children in audience

Dress up like character in the story

Representative animals and characters

Slides—homemade and otherwise

Recordings worked in with story

Finger plays and gestures

Series of standups

Book illustrations for story

Have other people sketch as you tell

T.V. or radio script (People act out while story is told)

Creative dramatics

Choral reading

Opaque projector

Well-done book review

Picture for background—on easel or otherwise
Centerpiece appropriate to story
Group participation
Finger painting
Clay manipulations
Shadowgraph
Voice variations
Scissor cutouts
Have children imitate sounds
Hand puppets
Chalk talk
Stick people sketches
Sound effects
Dialects
Wire recordings
Pantomime and have guess
Spontaneous dialogue
Developing characters with pipe cleaners
Maps appropriate to story
Live animals

Title: **ETHNIC, CULTURAL, AND PERSONAL STORY REFERENCES**

		Grade Level
Appearance—Fat		
Englebretson, Betty	"What Happened to George?"	1-2
Evers, Helen and Alf	"Plumo Pig"	1
Appearance—Size		
Bien, Jerrole	"Smallest Boy in the Class"	1-2
Felt, Sue	"Rosa-Too-Little"	K-1
Krasilovsky, Phyllis	"Very Little Girl"	K-1
Lipkind, William	"Even Steven"	K-3
Ward, Lynd	"Biggest Bear"	K-3
Traits of Character—Timidity		
Williams, Swenaira	"Timid Timothy"	1-2
Traits of Character—Greediness		
Riokind, William	"Finders Keepers"	K-3
Traits of Character—Accepting Responsibility		
Beskow, Elza	"Palle's New Suit"	1-2
Family Relationships—Everyday Life		
Lenski, Lois	"Papa Small"	K-2
Family Relationships—New Baby, Twins		
Flack, Marjorie	"New Pet"	1
Hawkins, Quaill	"Best Birthday"	K-2

Persons of Different Races and from Different Countries

Bannon, Laura	"Hat for a Hero" (Mexican)	1-3
Beim, Lorraine	"Two Is a Team" (Black)	1-2
Bemelmans, Ludwig	"Madeline's Rescue" (French)	1-3
Bontemps, Arna	"Lonesome Boy" (Black)	1-3
Flack, Marjorie	"Story About Ping" (Chinese)	1-3
Liang, Yen	"Dee Bee's Birthday" (Chinese)	K-1
Long, Eula	"Faraway Holiday" (Mexican)	1-2
Politi, Leo	"Little Leo" (Italian)	K-3

Blacks

Keats, Ezra Jack. *Whistle for Willie.* Viking Press, 1964. K-2

Konkle, Janet. *Schoolroom Bunny.* Childrens Press, 1965. K-1

Keats, Ezra Jack. *Snowy Day.* Viking Press, 1962. K-1

Stanek, Muriel. *One, Two, Three for Fun.* Albert Whitman K-3
and Company, 1966.

Gary, Janice May. *What May Jo Shared.* Albert Whitman K-3
and Company, 1967.

Vogel, Else-Margaret. *Hello Henry.* Parents Magazine Press, K-2
1965.

Wilson, Julia. *Becky.* Thomas Y. Crowell Company, 1966. K-3

Black American Poets (for elementary grades):

1. Gwendolyn Brooks
2. Paul Lawrence Dunbar
3. Langston Hughes
4. James Weldon Johnson
5. Phyllis Wheatly
6. Beatrice M. Murphy
7. Georgia Douglas Johnson
8. Fenton Johnson
9. Lewis Alexander
10. Countee Cullen
11. James David Dorrothers

Write:

Friendship Press
475 Riverside Drive
New York, New York 10027
for portraits of outstanding Blacks. $1.75 for 24 pictures, 11" x 14".

Filmstrip:

Robert and His Family. Four sound filmstrips; integrated. K-3
(available from FWCS Service Center). Fort Wayne, Indiana.

Film:

Skippy Learns a Lesson. K-3 (from FWCS Service Center)

Book:
Before WE Read. K-1 Readiness. Scott, Foresman & Company.

Indian (American):
Anasi the Spider, by Gerald McDermott. Holt, Rinehart and Winston, 1972.
Red Fox and His Canoe by Nathaniel Benchly. Harper & Row, 1964.
Indian Two Feet and His Eagle Feather by Margaret Friskey. Children's Press, 1967.
Indian Summer, by F. Monjo. Harper & Row, 1968.
The Magic Tree, by Gerald McDermott. Holt, Rinehart and Winston, 1973.

Japanese:
Timinoto's Great Adventure by Frank Francis. Holiday House, 1969.
Circus Day in Japan by Eleanor Hicks. Tuttle, 1953.
A Pair of Red Clogs by Maska Matsume. World, 1960.
Wieko by Leo Politi. Golden Gate Junior Books, 1969.
Moma's Kitten by Mitsu Yashima. Viking Press, 1961.
Crow Boy by Mitsu Yashima. Viking Press, 1955.

Everyone's Books, Easy Picture Books:
Just One Me, Aleen Brothers. Fowlett, 1967.
Goggles by Ezra Jack Keats. Macmillan, 1969.
Where Does the Day Go by Walter Myers. Parent's, 1969.

Books by Ezra Jack Keats:
   Hi Cat. Macmillan, 1969.
   Jennie's Hat. Harper & Row, 1966.
   A Letter to Amy. Harper & Row, 1966.
   Pet Show. Macmillan, 1972.
   Peter's Chair. Harper & Row, 1967.
   Snowy Day. Viking Press, 1962.
   Whistle for Willie. Viking Press, 1962.

Mexican-American:
Bad Boy, Good Boy by Marie Hall Ets. Thomas Y. Crowell, 1967.
Nine Days to Christmas by Marie Hall Ets. Viking Press, 1959.
Juanita by Leo Politi. Scribner's, 1948.

Chinese:
The Chinese Children Next Door by Pearl Buck. Day, 1969.

Nai Li by Thomas Handforth. Doubleday, 1938.
Chinese by Robert Wyndham. World, 1968.

Sound Filmstrips:
Joey's Cat, Robert Burch. Viking Press.
Peter's Chair, Ezra Jack Keats. Weston Woods.
Snowy Day, Ezra Jack Keats. Weston Woods.

Records:
African Folk Tales, Audio Visuals International.

Pictures:
Black ABC. SVE.

Title: **BOOKS AND STORIES**

Here is a list of children's books that can be purchased in bookstores. The books are arranged in descriptive categories.

POP-UPS—BOOKS WITH MOVABLE PARTS:

The Three Little Pigs	Retold by Albert G. Miller, de-
Hansel and Gretel	signed by Paul Taylor, illustrated
Little Red Riding Hood	by Gwen Gordon. Random House,
The Emperor's New Clothes	Inc., 1971. Price: $1.95

What Happens Next? (Pull tab to see result of action)
The Alphabet Book
(Sesame Street) Random House in conjunction with Children's Television Workshop. Price: $2.50.

The Pop-Up Color Book	
The Pop-Up Tournament of Magic	
Pop-Up Barbar's Games	
Pop-Up Biggest Book	Random House
Pop-Up Sound Alikes	Price: $2.50
Pop-Up Noah and the Ark	
Pop-Up the Night Before Christmas	
Pop-Up Mother Goose	
The Pop-Up Book of Left and Right	
Pop-Up Going to the Hospital	
Bennett Cerf's Pop-Up Limericks	

ROUNDED CORNERS AND THICK LAMINATED PAGES:

Little Turtle's Big Adventures by David Harrison. Illustrated by J. P. Miller. A Random House Early Bird Book, New York, 1969. Price: $1.95

Somebody Hides	
Nursery Rhymes	Golden Press
A Good, Good Morning	Western Publishing Company
The Color Train	New York, 1971. Price: $1.00
My Counting Book	

BOOKS THAT FLOAT: (For bathtub time)

Bubble Fun

Scrub-A-Dub (About a boy and a seal)

Platt and Munk, Publishers, Bronx, New York, Division of Questor Educational Products Company. Price: $1.95.

Waterproof pages, very colorful, two animal sponges on the back.

CLASSIC STORIES, WELL ILLUSTRATED:

Peter Pan

Walt Disney's Books, pictures by Walt Disney Studio 1950 copyright, 1971 printing, beautiful color. Price: $1.00.

Wilson's World by Edith Thacher Hurd, pictures by Clement Hurd. Harper and Row Publishers, New York, 1971. Price: $4.50. About a little boy who likes to paint and what he paints; beautiful color.

The Runaway Bunny by Margaret Wise Brown, pictures by Clement Hurd. Harper and Row Publishers, New York. Original copyright 1942, rewritten 1970, this printing 1972. Price: $3.95.

Puppy Dog Tales selected by Nita Jones, pictures by Dale Maxey. Random House. Large book, large print. Price: $1.50.

Turnabout by Munro Leaf.

J. B. Lippincott Company, Philadelphia, 1967. Price: $3.75. About a little boy's dream and whether it is real or not.

Let's Go to the Circus by Tony Palazzo.

Doubleday and Company, Inc., Garden City, New York, 1961. Price: $4.95.

Mike Mulligan and His Steam Shovel, story and pictures by Virginia Lee Burton. The Riverside Press–Cambridge. Houghton Mifflin Company, Boston, MA, 1939. Price: $3.75.

Fish Is Fish　　　　　　　　by Leo Lionni, Pantheon
Swimmy　　　　　　　　　Book, A Division of Random
Tico and the Golden Wings　House big books, large pictures,
　　　　　　　　　　　　　　Price: $3.95.
Frederick About a little mouse
The Biggest House in the World Written from a snail's point of
view.
Alexander and the Wind Up Mouse About a friendship between
a real and mechanical mouse.
The Alphabet Tree
Theodore and the Talking Mushroom Theodore is a mouse
One Day Everything Went Wrong by Elizabeth Vreeken, illus-
trated by Leonard Shortall. Young Readers Press, Inc., New
York, 1966. Price: 50 cents (paperback)
The Carrot Seed by Ruth Krauss, pictures by Crocket Johnson.
Scholastic Book Services, a division of Scholastic Magazines,
Inc. About a little boy who plants a carrot seed and watches it
grow.
Angus and the Cat by Marjorie Flack.
Young Readers Press, Inc., New York, 2nd printing, 1971. Price
95 cents. About a little boy named Angus and how he first
learns what a cat is.
The Little Island by Golden MacDonald, illustrations by Leonard
Weisgard. Doubleday and Company, Inc., Garden City, New
York. 2nd printing, 1971. Price: 95 cents.

FUTURISTIC TYPE:

　Land of Red　　　　　　by Peter Max
　Land of Yellow　　　　　Franklin Watts, Inc., 1970.
　These two books are about the colors in their titles presented in
　very modern psychedelic pictures.

NURSERY RHYMES

　One Fine Day by Nonny Hogrogian.
　The Macmillan Company/Collier-Macmillan LTD., London, 1971.
　Price: $4.95.
　Ten Little Foxes　　　　published by Brimax Books,
　Ten Little Kittens　　　　London. Price: $1.95.

FINGER PUPPET TYPE

　Funny Fingers by Kent Salisbury, pictures by Joan Allen. Golden
　Book, New York, Western Publishing Company, Inc., 1969.
　Price: $3.95.　　　　　　　78

Is This the House of Mistress Mouse? by Richard Scarry. Golden Book, Western Publishing Company, New York. Price: $2.50.

TOUCH

The Touch Me Book
A Golden Answer Book, Western Publishing Company, Inc. Price: $2.50.

SMELL

Little Bunny Follows His Nose
Detective Arthur on the Scent
Golden Books, Western Publishing Company, 1971. Price: $2.95. Each book has six different pieces depictive of the thing they smell like; you scratch the piece and smell your finger to see what it is.

PHOTOGRAPHS

The Red Balloon by A. Lamorisse.
Doubleday and Company, Inc., Garden City, New York, 1956. About the travels of a red balloon and the children who try to catch it.
The Lonely Doll. Story and photos by Dave Wright.
Doubleday and Company, Inc., Garden City, New York, 1957.

Farm Friends	Golden Books, by Shiba
Pets and Pals	Productions, LTD. in Japan,
Animal Babies	1971. Price: $1.00.

CHANGING PICTURE BOOKS

Children Here, Children There	by Leslie Burton, printed and
Nature's Helpers	bound in Japan for Child Guid-
Parade of Seasons	ance Products, Inc., Bronx, New
Numbers Are Things	York. Price: $3.00.
Up and Down and All	
Around	

BOOK WITH RECORD

The Six Button Dragon	by Matt Robinson, illustrated by
The Pecan Tree	Brumsic Brandon, Jr., narrated
A Lot of Hot Water	by Gordon of Sesame Street,
	45 r.p.m. Price: $1.95.

CONCEPT BOOKS

The Animals A, B, C's by Dean Walley, illustrated by Rich

Ruddish. Hallmark Cards, Kansas City, Missouri, printed in Singapore. Price: $3.50.

One Two Three (Learning to Count), illustrated by John Alcorn. Hallmark Cards, Kansas City, Missouri, printed in U.S. Price: $1.50.

Seal on Wheels by Dean Walley, illustrated by Michele Shulte. Hallmark Cards, Kansas City, Missouri, printed in U.S. Price: $2.50.

What Can You Feel With Your Feet? by Hertha Klugman, pictures by Frank E. Aloise.

What Happens to a Drink of Water? by Mary Elting, pictures by Cynthia and Alvin Koehler.

How Many Legs, How Many Toes by Mary Elting, pictures by Mac Conner.

Why Can't You See the Wind? by Sally Cartwright, pictures by William Plummer.

Happy, Sad, Silly, Mad by Barbara Shook Hazen, pictures by Elizabeth Dauber. Preschool Easy Answer Books. Price: $1.00.

Wild Animals and Their Babies by Jan Pfloog. Golden Book, Western Publishing Company, Inc. Price: $3.95.

Great Big Air Book by Richard Scarry, Random
Great Big Mystery Book House, New York, 1971. Price:
Great Big School House $3.95. Large books with large
ABC Word Book print

Sometimes I Get Angry by Jane Werner Watson, Robert E. Switzer,
Sometimes I'm Afraid M. D., and J. Cotter Huschberg,
  M. D., illustrations Hilde Hoffman

A Golden Book in conjunction with the Menninger Foundation for solving problems of childhood. Golden Press, New York, Western Publishing Company, Inc., 1971. Price: $1.95.

The Sesame Street Book of Shapes
The Sesame Street Book of Numbers
The Sesame Street Book of People and Things
The Sesame Street Story Book

Random House, Children's Television Workshop, 1971. Price: $3.95. Illustrated very well with color and action.

Hailstones and Halibut Bones by Mary O'Neill, illustrated by Leonard Weisgard. Doubleday and Company, Inc., Garden City, New York, 1961. Price: $3.95.

Takes the child on an adventure in color, answers questions such as What is white? and What is gold? by pictures.